A MEDIEVAL
FLOWER GARDEN

CHRONICLE BOOKS
SAN FRANCISCO

First published in the United States by Chronicle Books.

Copyright ©1994 by Pavilion Books, Ltd.
All rights reserved. No part of this book may be reproduced
without written permission from the Publisher.

Jacket design: Laura Lovett
Calligraphy: Georgia Deaver
Printed in Singapore.

Library of Congress Cataloging-in-Publication Data
A Medieval flower garden.
    72 p.   122 x 155mm
    ISBN 0-8118-0769-X
    1. Gardens, Medieval—Miscellanea. 2. Gardens—Gift books.
3. Flowers—Gift books.
    SB458.35.M44   1995
    712'.09'02—dc20   94-12326
                          CIP

Distributed in Canada by Raincoast Books,
112 East 3rd Avenue, Vancouver, B.C. V5T 1C8

10 9 8 7 6 5 4 3 2 1

Chronicle Books
275 Fifth St.
San Francisco, CA 94103

INTRODUCTION

I N THE MEDIEVAL WORLD FLOWERS WERE A SOURCE OF
delight. A fascination with flowers is evident in written
allusions and in the way that manuscript illuminations,
miniatures, and tapestries depict flowering trees and
wildflowers as well as more stylized plants. These sources
provide vital insights into what plants were available and
how they were grown.

Many plants of the medieval world are recognizable as
those grown in gardens today. In medieval images – as
now – primroses and cowslips herald spring, followed by
daffodils, periwinkle and violets. Plum, pear, and apple
trees blossom overhead, while wild strawberry, daisies,
and buttercups stud the ground below. The seasons
unfold with columbine, roses, Solomon's seal, yellow
water-flag, golden broom, and everlasting pea. Some of
these plants were natives that crept into gardens from the
surrounding countryside: the late-15th century *Hours of
Anne of Brittany*, the masterpiece of Jean Bourdichon,
court painter to the kings of France, contains three
hundred species, mostly found in the gardens, fields, and
woodlands of Touraine. Other plants (like hollyhocks,

lilies, and carnations) were exotics, treasured in the protected environment of gardens.

We grow many of these plants for their beauty or scent; different distinctions prevailed some thousand years ago. Growing food crops and herbs was a necessity of life, and almost all the flowering plants grown possessed culinary, medicinal, or herbal properties. Spiritual significance suffused this practical usefulness. The beauty and utility of flowers were taken as evidence of God's works, and individual flowers were imbued with symbolic significance. This is suggested in one of the earliest surviving plant lists – the Capitulare of about AD 800, in which essential plants to be cultivated in the gardens of Charlemagne's empire were specified. The first flowers mentioned are lilies and roses. Their position in the list must have been for religious reasons – the white lily symbolized the Virgin's purity and roses stood for the blood of martyrdom – but their presence in gardens had another, more down-to-earth cause: they were useful. The bulbs of madonna lilies were eaten as a food crop, but were used later as a salve. Roses have purgative properties and yielded scented petals for strewing and flavouring.

The art of gardening began to thrive in areas where relative political stability succeeded bitter feudal warfare, and the nobility no longer needed to protect themselves with fortifications and moats. Palaces and houses could be built in more hospitable terrain. As well as enclosures close to castle walls, more extensive areas of land could be turned into orchards or parkland.

The existence of gardens created for pleasure is documented in bills, lists, and written descriptions, but no accurate representations survive; handed down are the idealized or imagined views shown in paintings or in the miniatures from surviving manuscripts. This wealth of illustrations helps us to picture what they might have looked like. Similarly, written accounts of gardens occasionally mention some earthy detail that strikes a chord. Walafrid Strabo wrote his Latin poem *The Little Garden (Hortulus)* over a thousand years ago, but his description of his struggles with nettles and moles in a monastic garden is still vivid today. Other writers like Petrus de Crescentiis in his influential *Liber Ruralium Commodorum* lacked such an authentic voice of experience but concentrated more on ideas on style.

Certain themes from such writings appear again and again in medieval illustrations. In the foreground, beneath the house, appears an enclosure or 'herber'; outside might be a larger garden area, and farther off still, an orchard with walks and pools. In the background to other herbers we glimpse a wider tree-studded countryside which was orchard, pleasaunce, park, or hunting ground. Often the park would be filled with deer or more exotic animals. It might contain a pavilion or gloriette for viewing sports like archery, jousting, or hunting.

It is in the inner gardens that flowers are most in evidence. There are early references to gardens within castle and monastery walls. These were generally divided into a series of beds, often edged with timber or brick, and separated by paths of sand or gravel. The flower content of some beds was sparse, with plants dotted about in bare soil among tiered topiary bushes, in a style that we may find austere and artificial today.

Allowing for the fairytale architecture and the period costume, there is much that we can identify with in the illustrations of small gardens tucked in beside buildings or within castle precincts. Their geometric shape, their scale and their proximity to dwellings is something very familiar to 20th-century town gardeners. These gardens have an intimate, secluded atmosphere. They are framed by low fences or hedges and screening trelliswork, which is often clothed in climbers. Overhead plant-clad arbours and vines provide shelter and shade. The overall impression is of people enjoying their garden – they sit on benches or soft seats of turf. They are soothed by the sound of fountains and birdsong whilst perfumed flowers and aromatic leaves yield scents: these were gardens for all the senses.

If the images give us engaging insights into typical gardens of the period, their richness for the medieval eye lay in a different dimension. To a contemporary, everything would be charged with hidden meaning. Portrayals of the Virgin in a secret inner garden (the *hortus conclusus*) evoked the Biblical image of the Song of Songs, with the enclosure symbolizing Mary's intact purity and the garden's abundance corresponding to the flowers of virtue. The fountains that we see as ornamental features were equally symbolic – the Virgin is described as the 'fountain of gardens' and Dante called her a 'fountain of living things'. Like a fountain, her presence washed away sins and brought a state of grace.

The medieval cult of the Virgin led to the creation of 'Mary gardens' planted with significant flowers. More than twelve flowers were dedicated to the Virgin, among them marigolds, violets, and daisies. The latter was also called *herba trinitas*, since its three-coloured petals symbolized the Trinity, while field daisies or marguerites were sometimes called *oculis Christi* or 'eye of Christ'.

Iconography of medieval paintings often associates the Virgin with roses, or shows rosebuds in the garden of Paradise. 'Mary, the rose, was white through her virginity, red through her charity ... white by her love of God and red by her compassion,' in St Bernard's words. The rose was probably the most popular medieval flower and according to Bartholomaeus, 'among all flowers of the world the flower of the rose is the chief and beareth the prize.' As a symbol of martyrdom, the rose was also associated with Christ. As Walafrid Strabo wrote, he 'coloured roses by his death.'

The choice of texts included in this selection echoes the symbolism of the flowers. Beginning with an interpretation of the Garden of Eden, through visions of Earthly Paradise, to the Celestial Garden where the Virgin Mary and Christ are to be found, the blend of the spiritual and earthly reflects the popular beliefs of medieval times.

In the later Middle Ages the *hortus conclusus* came to represent the Virgin's purity; earlier interpretations equated the enclosed garden with the body of Christ and his Holy Church. This connection is traced back to early Persian gardens – precious enclosures representing the innermost joys of paradise amid an arid and dangerous desert landscape. The Persian *paradesios* which gave us the word paradise, is translated in Old Saxon and Anglo-Saxon texts as 'meadow', 'pasture' and, in one case, 'field of bliss'. The purpose of these gardens was to enchant the spirit and to aim for ultimate perfection – but not to confuse earthly delights with heaven, the ultimate goal. The sophisticated garden skills of Islam were already highly developed when Christian soldiers on crusades in the 12th century first beheld splendours beyond their imagination. Reports filtered back to the West of magical places with fountains and running water, flowering trees and singing birds. They were reminiscent of descriptions of the Garden of Eden, where it was always spring and the setting was a background for romance and dalliance. Plants and design influences percolated into the gardens emerging in north-western Europe via the Arab presence in Spain, Portugal, and Italy, but it was the spirit of these ideal gardens that captured the imagination, particularly of the poets.

Secular literature began to be circulated in the later Middle Ages, as copies of manuscripts started to reach a wider audience. The *Roman de la Rose*, begun by Guillaume de Lorris but completed by Jean de Meun, is perhaps the greatest allegory on a flower to have been written. It describes the lover's quest to find the rose with whose reflection he had fallen in love. Boccaccio, in his *Decameron*, and Geoffrey Chaucer both show considerable affection for flowers and gardens. These works were illustrated and produced by hand initially for noble families, but with the advent of printing, books reached a greater readership. One aspect of this development was that many more people could commission or engage in botanical research. John Gerard's *Herball*, although from a later Tudor period, is included in this selection as an example of the popular botanical writing, forming a bridge between the thinking of the Middle Ages and later scientific discoveries.

Fortunately for us, these verbal and visual pictures remain, conjuring up a time when the magic of the changing seasons and the beauty of the natural world were a great source of pleasure.

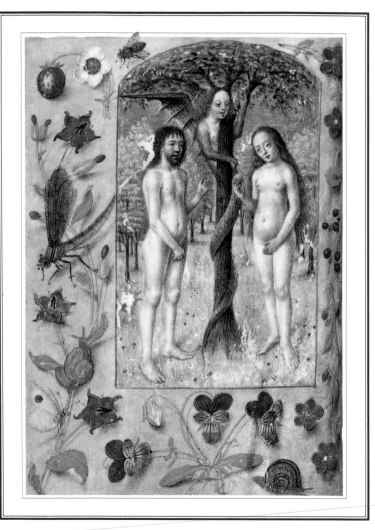

THE GARDEN OF EDEN

B UT ALSO CHOSE FOR HIM A HAPPY SEAT
A climate both for cold and heat,
Which dainty Flora paveth sumptuously
With flowery Ver's enamelled tapestry;
Pomona pranks with fruits, whose taste excels
And Zephyr fills with musk and amber smells;
Where God himself (as gardener) treads the alleys,
With trees and corn covers the hills and valleys;
Summons sweet sleep with noise of hundred brooks,
And sun-proof arbours makes in sundry nooks;
He plants, he proins, he pares, he trimmeth round
Th'evergreen beauties of a fruitfull ground;
Here-there the course of th' Holy Lakes he leads,
With thousand Dies he motleys all the Meades.

GUILLAUME DE SALUSTE *DU BARTAS*, 1581

ROSES AND LILIES

WHO CAN DESCRIBE THE EXCEEDING WHITENESS OF the lily? The rose, it should be crowned with pearls of Arabia and Lydian gold.

Better and sweeter are these flowers than all other plants and rightly called the flower of flowers. Yes, roses and lilies, the one for virginity with no sordid toil, no warmth of love, but the glow of their own sweet scent, which spreads further than the rival roses, but once bruised or crushed turns all to rankness. Therefore roses and lilies for our church, one for the martyr's blood, the other for the symbol in his hand. Pluck them, O maiden, roses for war and lilies for peace, and think of that Flower of the stem of Jesse. Lilies His words were, and the hallowed acts of His pleasant life, but His death re-dyed the roses.

WALAFRID STRABO, THE LITTLE GARDEN (HORTULUS), 9th century

A ROYAL GARDEN

OF THE GARDENS OF ROYAL PERSONAGES AND POWERFUL and wealthy lords.

And inasmuch as wealthy persons can by their riches and power obtain such things as please them and need only science and art to create all they desire.

For them, therefore, let a great meadow be chosen, arranged, and ordered, as here shall be directed. Let it be a place where the pleasant winds blow and where there are fountains of waters; it should be twenty 'Journaux' or more in size according to the will of the Lord and it should be enclosed with lofty walls. Let there be in some part a wood of divers trees where the wild beasts may find a refuge. In another part let there be a costly pavilion where the king and his queen or the lord or lady may dwell, when they wish to escape from wearisome occupations and where they may solace themselves.

PETRUS CRESCENTIIS, *OPUS RURALIUM COMMODORUM*, 1305

21

AN IDEAL GARDEN

L ET THERE BE SHADE AND LET THE WINDOWS OF THE pavilion look out upon the garden but not exposed to the burning rays of the sun. Let fish-pools be made and divers fishes placed therein. Let there also be hares, rabbits, deer and such-like wild animals that are not beasts of prey. And in the trees near the pavilion let great cages be made and therein place partridges, nightingales, blackbirds, linnets and all manner of singing birds. Let all be arranged so that the beasts and the birds may easily be seen from the pavilion.

Let there also be made a pavilion with rooms and towers wholly made of trees where the king, the queen or the lords and ladies may resort in fine weather. This pavilion may be made in this manner. The spaces and rooms may be measured out and where there would be walls there plant fruit-bearing trees which can easily be interlaced, such as cherries and apple-trees, or else olives or poplars which will grow quickly. Or this pavilion may more easily be made of dead wood and planted with vines which will cover the building. The trees may be grafted with divers fruit by the diligent gardener. It will be

needful for him to know all the different kinds of trees and herbs so that he may perform his work diligently and that no fault may be found by the king or lord.

When this work is accomplished then the king may delight himself in this garden, thanking and glorifying God the Sovereign Lord of all, the Cause and Author, the beginning and the end of all that is good.

PETRUS CRESCENTIIS, *OPUS RURALIUM COMMODORUM*, 1305

CORNE-ROSE OR WILDE POPPY

THE STALKS OF RED POPPY BE BLACKE, TENDER, AND brittle, somewhat hairy: the leaves are cut round about with deepe gashes like those of Succorie or wild Rocket. The flours grow forth at the tops of the stalks, being of a beautifull and gallant red colour, with blackish threds compassing about the middle part of the head, which being fully growne, is lesser than that of the garden Poppy: the seed is small and blacke.

The fields are garnished and overspred with these wilde Poppies in June and August.

Most men being led rather by false experiments than reason, commend the floures against the Pleurisie, giving to drinke as soon as the pain comes, either the distilled water, or syrup made by often infusing the leaves. And yet many times it happens, that the paine ceaseth by that meanes, though hardly sometimes.

JOHN GERARD, *THE HERBALL OR GENERALL HISTORIE OF PLANTES*, 1597

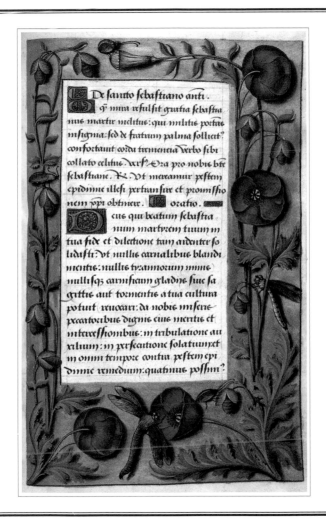

De sancto sebastiano anti.

O̅ nimia refulsit gratia sebastia
nus martir melitus: qui militie portans
insignia: sed de fratrum palma sollicit?
confortauit corda tormenta verbo sibi
collato celitus. xr̅s. Ora pro nobis b̅e
sebastiane. R̅. Vt mereamur pestem
epidimie illesi pertransire et promissio
nem xp̅i obtinere. Oratio.

Deus qui beatum sebastia
num martyrem tuum in
tua fide et dilectione tam ardenter so
lidasti: vt nullis carnalibus blandi
mentis: nullis tyrannorum minis
nullisq̅ carnificum gladiis siue sa
gittis aut tormentis a tua cultura
potuit reuocari: da nobis misere
peccatoribus dignis eius meritis et
intercessionibus: in tribulatione au
xilium: in persecutione solatium et
in omni tempore contra pestem epi
dimie remedium: quatinus possim?

A CASTLE GARDEN

Now was there made fast by the Towis wall,
A garden fair; and in the corners set
An arbour green, with wandis long and small
Railéd about and so with trées set
Was all the place, and Hawthorne hedges knet
That lyf was none walking there forbye
That might within scarce any wight espy,
So thick the boughes and the leaves green
Beshaded all the alleys that were there,
And mids of every arbour might be seen
The sharpe greene sweet Juniper
Growing so fair with branches here and there
That as it seemed to a lyf without,
The boughs spread the arbour all about.
And on the smalle greene twistis sat
The little sweet nightingale, and sung
So loud and clear, the hymnis consecrat
Of loris use, now soft, now loud, among,
That all the gardens and the wallis rung
Right of their song.

JAMES I OF SCOTLAND, THE KING'S QUAIR, written during
imprisonment at Windsor Castle, 1413-24

THE MYSTIC ROSE

I N FASHION THEN AS OF A SNOW-WHITE ROSE
  Displayed itself to me the saintly host,
    Whom Christ in his own blood had made his bride,
But the other host, that flying sees and sings
  The glory of Him who doth enamour it,
    And the goodness that created it so noble,
Even as a swarm of bees, that sinks in flowers
  One moment, and the next returns again
    To where its labour is to sweetness turned,
Sank into the great flower, that is adorned
  With leaves so many, and thence reascended
    To where its love abideth evermore.
Their faces had they all of living flame,
  And wings of gold, and all the rest so white
    No snow unto that limit doth attain.

From bench to bench, into the flower descending,
    They carried something of the peace and ardour
    Which by the fanning of their flanks they won.
Nor did the interposing 'twixt the flower
    And what was o'er it of such plenitude
    Of flying shapes impede the sight and splendour
Because the light divine so penetrates
    The universe, according to its merit,
    That naught can be an obstacle against it.

DANTE, *THE DIVINE COMEDY, IN PARADISO,* Canto XXXI,
13th century

THE LELY

T HE LELY IS AN HERBE WYTH A WHYTE FLOURE. AND
though the levys of the floure be whyte: yet wythin
shyneth the lykenesse of golde.

BARTHOLOMÆUS ANGLICUS, *DE PROPRIETATIBUS RERUM*, 1240

31

TO A LADY

S WEET ROIS¹ OF VERTEW AND OF GENTILNESS,
 Delystum lily of everie lustynes,
    Richest in bontie and in bewtie clear,
    And everie vertew that is wenit² dear,
Except onlie that ye are mercyless.

Into your garth³ this day I did persew;
There saw I flowris that fresche were of hew;
    Baith quhyte and reid most lusty were to seyne⁴,
    And halesome herbis upon stalkis greene;
Yet leaf nor flowr find could I nane of rew.

I doubt that Merche, with his cauld blastis keyne,
Has slain this gentil herb, that I of mene⁵;
    Quhois piteous death dois to my heart sic paine
    That I would make to plant his root againe, –
So confortand his levis unto me bene.

WILLIAM DUNBAR, 15th century

¹ rose. ² weened, esteemed. ³ garden-close. ⁴ to see.
⁵ that I complain of, mourn for.

32

CARNATION

THERE ARE AT THIS DAY UNDER THE NAME OF *Cariophyllus* comprehended divers and sundry sorts of plants, of such various colours, and also severall shapes, that a great and large volume would not suffice to write of every one at large in particular; considering how infinite they are, and how every yeare every clymate and country bringeth forth new sorts, such as have not heretofore been written of; some whereof are called Carnations, other Clove Gillofloures, some Sops in wine, some Pagiants, or Pagion color, Horse-flesh, blunket, purple, white, double and single Gilloifloures, as also a Gillofloure with yellow flours.

The great Carnation Gillo-floure hath a thick round wooddy root, from which riseth up many strong joynted stalks set with long green leaves by couples: on the top of the stalks do grow very fair floures of an excellent sweet smell, and pleasant Carnation colour, whereof it tooke his name.

JOHN GERARD, *THE HERBALL OR GENERALL HISTORIE OF PLANTES*, 1597

Incipiunt septem psalmi penitentia
les. Ant. Ne reminiscaris domine
Domine. psalm⁹
ne in furore tuo
arguas me neq;
in ira tua corripi
as me. Miserere mei domine
quoniam infirmus sum sana me
domine: quoniam conturbata sūt
omnia ossa mea. Et anima me
a turbata est ualde: sz tu domine us
q; quo. Conuertere domine 7
eripe animam meam. saluum me
fac ppter misericordiam tuam. o
Quoniam non est in morte qui
memor sit tui in inferno aūt quis
confitebitur tibi. Laboraui in
gemitu meo lauabo per singulas
noctes lectum meum lacrimis:

THE COLOURS OF FLORA

Then in we went, to the garden glorious
Like to a place, of pleasure most solacious
With Flora paynted and wrought curiously
In divers knottes of marveylous greatnes.
Rampande Lyons stode up wonderfly
Made all of herbes with dulcet swetenes,
With many dragons of marveylos likenes
Of divers floures made, full craftely
By Flora couloured, with colours sundrye.

Amiddes the garden so much delectable
There was an harber, fayre and quadrant
To Paradise, right well comparable
Set all about with floures fragrant,
And in the middle, there was resplenishaunt
A dulcet spring, and marveylous fountaine
Of gold and asure, made all certaine.

Stephen Hawes, *The Historie of graunde Amoure
and la bell Pucel*, 1554

A MAGICAL FOUNTAIN

.... WITHOUT THE DOOR
Of paradise the blest, I ween
No sight more beauteous may be seen
Than this bright well. The gushing source
Springs ever fresh and sweet. Its course
It takes through runnels twain, full deep,
And broadly trenched; it knows no sleep
By day or night, for ne'er 'tis dried
By wasting drought of summer tide,
Nor hath stern winter's iron hand
The power to make its waters stand
Immovable, but out the ground
Its babble calls, the whole year round
Close, tender herbage, which doth push
Unceasingly, strong, thick and lush.
Fast in the fountain's pavement shone
Two sparkling spheres of crystal stone,
Whereon my gaze with wonder fell. . .

GUILLAUME DE LORRIS AND JEAN DE MEUN
ROMAN DE LA ROSE, 13th century

Ser y fery et
furtar.
Et maintesfoie
le scontar
Se le oxxoye leane mille ame
Le truchet qui estoit de charme
Me ouvrit une pucelliette
Qui asser estoit comte et nette
Benault au blonc ceding bastl
La char plus tendre qui ii youfm

front reluifant fource; vouftie
Lentreoal fi neftout pas peue
Ainefur affermantey infume
Lenient bien fait a deoitture
Les reuls eut vos come saulante
Pour fure ennie aroudfioue
Doulce alame eut et fauouxe
La face blanche et coufource
La bouefe peute et tiaffette
Etau menton une foffette

39

Comment n̄ꝰ seigꝰ par son ange enuoia les trois fleurs de lis ꝓꝯ en vn escu de saur au roy clouꝭ.

THE LEGEND OF THE FLEURS DE LYS

THE FLOWER DE LUCE, OR FLEUR DE LYS (*IRIS pseudacorus*) is the origin of the heraldic emblem of the kings of France. Legend has it that in the 6th century, the Frankish king, Clovis, prayed for victory to the god of his Christian wife, Clothilde. Ensuing military success led to his becoming Christian and he replaced the three toads on his banner with three irises, the iris being one of the flowers of the Virgin. It was adopted by Louis VII in his Crusades, and became known as the fleur de Louis, thus fleur de lys (although another theory is that it is named after the river Lys, where it flowered profusely). In this depiction, the Almighty dispatched an angel to entrust the three fleurs de lys to a hermit who, in turn, gave them to Clothilde: she is seen handing them to Clovis on his conversion to Christianity. The allegory underlined Burgundian support for any claimant to the French crown: Henry V of England received the fleur de lys on his marriage to Catherine of France.

A MONASTERY GARDEN

To the beloved Father Grimaldus this small treatise is humbly offered by his obedient servant in token of love and admiration.

When you sit beneath the apple tree, where often you are surrounded by the boys from your school, some of them running to show you apples they have gathered so large they can scarcely hold them in one hand, perchance you will peruse it. May God make you abound more and more in goodness and crown you with life everlasting.

No joy is so great in a life of seclusion as that of gardening. No matter what the soil may be, sandy or heavy clay, on a hill or a slope, it will serve well. The gardener must not be slothful but full of zeal continuously, nor must he despise hardening his hands with toil.

When last winter had past and spring had renewed the face of the earth, when the days grew longer and milder, when flowers and herbs were stirred by the west wind, when green leaves clothed the trees, then my little plot was overgrown with nettles. What was I to do? Deep down the roots were matted and linked and riveted like

basket-work or the wattled hurdles of the fold. I prepare to attack, armed with the 'tooth of Saturn', tear up the clods and rend them from the clinging network of nettle-roots. Then I surround the space with a border of stout squared logs, piling the soil within to a convenient height, I spread manure on it. I plant my seeds and the kindly dew moistens them. Should drought prevail I must water it, letting the drops fall through my fingers for the impetus of a full stream from the water-pot would disturb my seedlings. Part of my garden is hard and dry under the shadow of a roof; in another part a high brick wall robs it of air and sun. Even here something will at least succeed.

WALAFRID STRABO, *THE LITTLE GARDEN* (*HORTULUS*), 9th century

WILDE ROSES

THE SWEET BRIER DOTH OFTENTIMES GROW HIGHER than all the kindes of Roses; the shoots of it are hard, thicke, and wooddy; the leaves are glittering, and of a beautifull greene colour, of smell most pleasant: the Roses are little, five leaved, most commonly whitish, seldom tending to purple, of little or no smell at all: the fruit is long, of colour somewhat red, like a little olive stone, & like the little heads or berries of the others, but lesser than those of the garden: in which is contained rough cotton, or hairy downe and seed, folded and wrapped up in the same, which is small and hard: there be likewise found about the slender shoots hereof, round, soft, and hairy spunges, which we call Brier Balls, such as grow about the prickles of the Dog-Rose.

We have in our London gardens another sweet Brier, having greater leaves, and much sweeter: the floures likewise are greater, and somewhat doubled, exceeding sweet of smell, wherein it differeth from the former.

JOHN GERARD, THE HERBALL OR GENERALL HISTORIE OF PLANTES, 1597

44

Ad nona
de bta
a
in.

GARDENS FOR STORYTELLING

THUS DISMISSED BY THEIR NEW QUEEN THE GAY company sauntered gently through a garden, the young men saying sweet things to the fair ladies, who wove fair garlands of divers sorts of leaves and sang love-songs.

Shortly after none[1] the queen rose, and roused the rest of the ladies, as also the young men, averring that it was injurious to the health to sleep long in the daytime. They therefore hied them to a meadow, where the grass grew green and luxuriant, being nowhere scorched by the sun, and a light breeze gently fanned them. So at the queen's command they all ranged themselves in a circle on the grass, and hearkened while she thus spoke:

'You mark that the sun is high, the heat intense, and the silence unbroken save by the cicalas among the olive-trees. It were therefore the height of folly to quit this spot at present. Here the air is cool and the prospect fair, and here, observe, are dice and chess. Take, then, your pleasure as you may be severally minded; but, if you take my advice, you will find pastime for the hot hours before us, not in play, in which the loser must needs be vexed,

and neither the winner nor the onlooker much the better
pleased, but in telling of stories, in which the invention of
one may afford solace to all the company of his hearers.'

BOCCACCIO, *THE DECAMERON*, 14th century

¹ The canonical hour following sext i.e. 3 p.m.

A GARDEN OF PLEASURE

CARE MUST BE TAKEN THAT THE LAWN IS OF SUCH A SIZE that about it in a square may be planted every sweet-smelling herb such as rue, and sage and basil, and likewise all sorts of flowers, as the violet, columbine, lily, rose, iris and the like. So that between these herbs and the turf, at the edge of the lawn set square, let there be a higher bench of turf flowering and lovely; and somewhere in the middle provide seats so that men may sit down there to take their repose pleasurably when their senses need refreshment. Upon the lawn too, against the heat of the sun, trees should be planted or vines trained, so that the lawn may have a delightful and cooling shade, sheltered by their leaves. For from these trees shade is more sought after than fruit, so that not much trouble should be taken to dig about and manure them, for this might cause great damage to the turf. Care should also be taken that the trees are not too close together or too numerous, for cutting off the breeze may do harm to health. The pleasure garden needs to have a free current of air along with shade. It also needs to be considered that the trees should not be bitter ones whose shade gives rise to

diseases, such as the walnut and some others; but let them be sweet trees, with perfumed flowers and agreeable shade, like grapevines, pears, apples, pomegranates, sweet bay trees, cypresses and such like.

ALBERTUS MAGNUS, *DE VEGETABILIBUS ET PLANTIS*, c.1260

A MYSTIC GARDEN

WITHIN THE GLADES SPRANG FOUNTAINS CLEAR;
No frog or newt e'er came anear
Their waters, but neath cooling shade
They gently sounded. Mirth had made
Therefrom small channelled brooks to fling
Their waves with pleasant murmuring
In tiny tides. Bright green and lush,
Around these sparkling streams did push
The sweetest grass . . .

.   .   .   .   .

The earth
Made pregnant by the streams gave birth
To thymy herbage and gay flowers,
And when drear winter frowns and lowers
In spots less genial, ever here
Things bud and burgeon through the year.
The violet, sweet of scent and hue,
The periwinkle's star of blue,
The golden kingcups burnished bright,
Mingled with pink-rimmed daisies white,
And varied flowers, blue, gold, and red,
The alleys, lawns and grooves o'erspread.
As they by Nature's craft had been
Enamelled deftly, on the green,
And all around where'er I went
Fresh blooms cast forth odorous scent.
Small need there is to fabulate
More fully of the fair estate
Of this most comely garden, lest
It weary your patience; nought expressed
Could all the glorious beauty be
Of this most wondrous place by me.

GUILLAUME DE LORRIS AND JEAN DE MEUN,
ROMAN DE LA ROSE, 13th century

GARDEN FAYRE

IN WONDERFULL AND CURIOUS SIMILITUDE
There stode a dragon, of fine gold so pure
Upon his tayle, of mighty fortitude
Wrethed and skaled, all wyth asure
Having thre heades, divers in figure
Whiche in a bathe, of the silver great
Spouted the water, that was so dulcet.

Beside whiche fountaine, the most fayre lady
La bell Pucell, was gayly sittyng
Of many floures, fayre and royally
A goodly chaplet, she was in makynge
Her heere was downe so clearely shinyng
Like to the golde, late purified with fire
Her heere was bryght, as the drawen wyre.

Like to a ladye, for to be right true
She ware a fayre, and goodly garment
Of most fine velvet, all of Indy blewe
With armines powdred, bordred at the vent,
On her fayre handes, as was convenient
A payre of gloves, right slender and soft
In approaching nere, I did beholde her oft.

STEPHEN HAWES, *THE HISTORIE OF GRAUNDE AMOURE AND LA BELL
PUCEL*, 1554

THE GARDEN IN SPRING

MAY HADDE PEYNTED WITH HIS SOFTÉ SHOWERS
This gardyn full of levés and of flowres;
And craft of manne's hand so curiously
Arrayéd hadde this gardyn trewély
That never was ther gardyn of swich prys,
But if it were the verray Paradys.
The odour of flowrés and the fresshé sighte
Wolde han makéd any herté lighte
That ever was born, but if to greet siknesse,
Or too greet sorwé, helde it in distresse;
So full it was of beautee with plesance.

GEOFFREY CHAUCER, *THE FRANKLIN'S TALE*, 1386-7

LILLY IN THE VALLEY, OR MAY LILLY

THE CONVALL LILLY, OR LILLY OF THE VALLY, HATH many leaves like the smallest leaves of Water Plantaine; among which riseth up a naked stalke halfe a foot high, garnished with many white floures like little bels, with blunt and turned edges, of a strong savour, yet pleasant enough; which being past, there come small red berries, much like the berries of *Asparagus*, wherein the seed is contained. The root is small and slender creeping far abroad in the ground.

The second kinde of May Lillies is like the former in every respect; and herein varieth or differeth, in that this kinde hath reddish floures, and is thought to have the sweeter smell.

The Latines have named it *Lilium Convallium*: in French, *Muguet*: yet there is likewise another herbe which they call *Muguet*, commonly named in English, Woodroof. It is called in English, Lilly of the Valley, or the Convall Lillie, and May Lillies, and in some places Liriconfancie.

The floures of the Valley Lillie distilled with wine, and drunke the quantitie of a spoonefull, restore speech unto those that have the dumb palsie and that are falne into

the Apoplexie, and are good against the gout, and comfort the heart.

The water aforesaid doth strengthen the memory that is weakened and diminished; it helpeth also the inflammations of the eies, being dropped thereinto.

The floures of May Lillies put into a glasse, and set in a hill of ants, close stopped for the space of a moneth, and then taken out, therein you shall finde a liquor that appeaseth the paine and griefe of the gout, being outwardly applied; which is commended to be most excellent.

JOHN GERARD, *THE HERBALL OR GENERALL HISTORIE OF PLANTES,*
1597

ROSES

THE ROSE OF YE GARDEN AND THE WYLDE ROSE BEN dyvers in multitude of floures: smelle and colour: and also in vertue. For the leves of the wylde rose ben fewe and brode and whytyssh: meddlyd wyth lytyll rednesse: and smellyth not so wel as the tame rose. Nother is so vertuous in medicyn. The tame rose hath many levys sette nye togyder; and ben all red other almost white: w' wonder good smell. . . . And the more they ben brused and broken: the vertuouser they ben and the better smellynge. And springeth out of a thorne that is harde and rough: netheles the Rose folowyth not the Kynde of the thorne: But she arayeth her thorn wyth fayr colour and good smell. Whan ye rose begynneth to sprynge it is closed in a Knoppe wyth grenes: and that Knoppe is grene. And whane it swellyth thenne spryngeth out harde levys and sharpe. . . . And whane they ben full growen they sprede theymselves agenst the sonne rysynge. And for they ben tendre and feble to holde togyder in the begynnynge theyfore about those smale grene levys ben nyghe the red and tendre levys. And ben sette all aboute. And in the mydill thereof is seen the sede small and yellow wyth full

gode smell. . . . Among all floures of the worlde the floure of the rose is chief and beeryth ye pryse. And by cause of vertues and swete smelle and savour. For by fayrnesse they fede the syghte; and playseth the smelle by odour, the touche by softe handlynge. And wythstondeth and socouryth by vertue agenst many syknesses and evylles.

BARTHOLOMAEUS ANGLICUS, *DE PROPRIETATIBUS RERUM*, 1240

A SYMBOLIC CASTLE

A GARDEN SPIED I, GREAT AND FAIR,
The which a castled wall hemmed round
The wall was high, and built of hard
Rough stone, close shut, and strongly barred,
Hot-foot, the boundary's full extent
I traversed, heart and soul intent
Some aperture to spy; at last
Mine eye with eager joy I cast
Upon a wicket, straight, and small
Worked in the stern forbidding wall,
And forthwith set myself to get
An entry there, whate'er might let.

Full many a time with sounding blow
I struck the door, and, head bent low,
Stood hearkening who might make reply.
The horn-beam wicket presently
Was opened by a dame of air
Most gracious, and of beauty rare.

GUILLAUME DE LORRIS AND JEAN DE MEUN,
ROMAN DE LA ROSE, 13th century

THE GARDEN OF GETHSEMANE

AND HE CAME OUT, AND WENT, AS HE WAS WONT, TO the mount of Olives; and his disciples also followed him.

And when he was at the place, he said unto them, Pray that ye enter not into temptation.

And he was withdrawn from them about a stone's cast, and kneeled down, and prayed.

Saying, Father, if thou be willing, remove this cup from me: nevertheless not my will, but thine, be done.

And there appeared an angel unto him from heaven, strengthening him.

And being in an agony he prayed more earnestly: and his sweat was as it were great drops of blood falling down to the ground.

And when he rose up from prayer, and was come to his disciples, he found them sleeping for sorrow.

THE GOSPEL ACCORDING TO ST. LUKE, XXII, 39-45

VIOLETS

VIOLET IS A LITTLE HEARBE IN SUBSTANCE, AND IS better fresh and newe, then when it is olde, and the flowre thereof smelleth most, and so the smell thereof abateth heate of the braine, and refresheth and comforteth the spirites of feeling, and maketh sleepe, for it cooleth and tempereth and moysteneth the braine: and the more vertuous the flowre thereof is the more it bendeth the head thereof downward.

Also flowres of springing time spring first and sheweth Summer. The lyttlenesse thereof in substance is noblye rewarded in greatnesse of savour and of vertue.

BARTHOLOMAEUS ANGLICUS, *DE PROPRIETATIBUS RERUM*, 1240

Ad matutinas
de sancto
spiri-
tu.

THE CELESTIAL GARDEN

'OF WHATSOEVER THINGS I HAVE BEHELD,
   As coming from thy power and from thy goodness
   I recognise the virtue and the grace.
Thou from a slave hast brought me unto freedom.
   By all those ways, by all the expedients,
   Whereby thou hadst the power of doing it.
Preserve towards me thy magnificence,
   So that this soul of mine, which thou hast healed,
   Pleasing to thee be loosened from the body.'
Thus I implored; and she, so far away,
   Smiled, as it seemed, and looked once more at me:
   Then unto the eternal fountain turned.
And said the Old Man holy: 'That thou mayst
   Accomplish perfectly thy journeying,
   Whereunto prayer and holy love have sent me,
Fly with thine eyes all round about this garden;
   For seeing it will discipline thy sight
   Farther to mount along the ray divine.
And she, the Queen of Heaven, for whom I burn
   Wholly with love, will grant us every grace,
   Because that I her faithful Bernard am.'

As he who peradventure from Croatia
    Cometh to gaze at our Veronica,
    Who through its ancient fame is never sated,
But says in thought, the while it is displayed,
    'My Lord, Christ Jesus, God of very God,
    Now was your semblance made like unto this!'
Even such was I while gazing at the living
    Charity of the man, who in this world
    By contemplation tasted of that peace.

DANTE, *THE DIVINE COMEDY*, *IN PARADISO*, Canto XXXI,
13th century

Acknowledgements

Text acknowledgements:

Extracts from the Authorised version of the Bible (The King James Bible), the rights in which are vested in the Crown, are reproduced by permission of the Crown's Patentee, Cambridge University Press.

The extract from Boccaccio's Decameron is reproduced by kind permission of Everyman's Library, David Campbell Publishers Ltd.

Picture credits:

Biblioteca Casanatense, Rome Cover, 5, 59: *Tacuinum Sanitatis f. LXIX*

Biblioteca Nazionale Marciana, Venice 31: *MS Lat 1, 99, f. 831r*

Bodleian Library, Oxford 47: *MS Douce 213 f. 1*, 50: *MS Douce FF 59 f. 161*, 57: *MS Douce FF 59 f. 114*, 62: *MS Douce 256 f. 19v*

Bridgeman Art Library/British Library 25: *Add MS 18855 f. 103*, 45: *Add MS 35214 f. 67*, 65: *Add MS 35214 ffs 49b-50*

Bridgeman Art Library/Osterreichisches Nationalbibliothek 33

British Library, London 7: *MS Sloane 4016 f.30*, 19: *Add MS 54782 f. 265b*, 20: *Add MS 19720 f. 27*, 23: *MS Egerton 3781 f. 1r*, 26: *MS Harley 4431 f. 376*, 29: *Yates Thompson MS 36 f. 185*, 30: *Add MS 35314 f. 12v*, 35: *Add MS 38126 f. 110*, 36: *MS Royal 6 E IX, f. 15v*, 39: *MS Harley 4425 f. 12v*, 40: *Add MS 18850 f. 288v*, 43: *Add MS 19720 f. 10*, 49: *MS Royal 6E IX, f. 15v*, 61: *MS Harley 4425 f. 39*, 67: *Yates Thompson MS 36, f. 186*

Giraudon/Bibliothèque de l'Arsenal, Paris 53: *MS 5072 f. 71v*

Giraudon/Museé Condé, Chantilly 4: *MS 340/603*

Library of Congress, Washington, Rare Book Collection 16: *MS 139*

Scala/Castello del Buonconsiglio Trent 55